Name of Business _____

Address of Business _____

Telephone No. _____

Log No. _____

Start Date _____

End Date _____

Notes

_____
_____
_____
_____
_____
_____
_____
_____
_____
_____
_____
_____
_____
_____
_____

Date	Visitor's Name	Time In	Time Out	Reason for Visit	Signature

Date	Visitor's Name	Time In	Time Out	Reason for Visit	Signature

Date	Visitor's Name	Time In	Time Out	Reason for Visit	Signature

Date	Visitor's Name	Time In	Time Out	Reason for Visit	Signature

Date	Visitor's Name	Time In	Time Out	Reason for Visit	Signature

Date	Visitor's Name	Time In	Time Out	Reason for Visit	Signature

Date	Visitor's Name	Time In	Time Out	Reason for Visit	Signature

Date	Visitor's Name	Time In	Time Out	Reason for Visit	Signature

Date	Visitor's Name	Time In	Time Out	Reason for Visit	Signature

Date	Visitor's Name	Time In	Time Out	Reason for Visit	Signature

Date	Visitor's Name	Time In	Time Out	Reason for Visit	Signature

Date	Visitor's Name	Time In	Time Out	Reason for Visit	Signature

Date	Visitor's Name	Time In	Time Out	Reason for Visit	Signature

Date	Visitor's Name	Time In	Time Out	Reason for Visit	Signature

Date	Visitor's Name	Time In	Time Out	Reason for Visit	Signature

Date	Visitor's Name	Time In	Time Out	Reason for Visit	Signature

Date	Visitor's Name	Time In	Time Out	Reason for Visit	Signature

Date	Visitor's Name	Time In	Time Out	Reason for Visit	Signature

Date	Visitor's Name	Time In	Time Out	Reason for Visit	Signature

Date	Visitor's Name	Time In	Time Out	Reason for Visit	Signature

Date	Visitor's Name	Time In	Time Out	Reason for Visit	Signature

Date	Visitor's Name	Time In	Time Out	Reason for Visit	Signature

Date	Visitor's Name	Time In	Time Out	Reason for Visit	Signature

Date	Visitor's Name	Time In	Time Out	Reason for Visit	Signature

Date	Visitor's Name	Time In	Time Out	Reason for Visit	Signature

Date	Visitor's Name	Time In	Time Out	Reason for Visit	Signature

Date	Visitor's Name	Time In	Time Out	Reason for Visit	Signature

Date	Visitor's Name	Time In	Time Out	Reason for Visit	Signature

Date	Visitor's Name	Time In	Time Out	Reason for Visit	Signature

Date	Visitor's Name	Time In	Time Out	Reason for Visit	Signature

Date	Visitor's Name	Time In	Time Out	Reason for Visit	Signature

Date	Visitor's Name	Time In	Time Out	Reason for Visit	Signature

Date	Visitor's Name	Time In	Time Out	Reason for Visit	Signature

Date	Visitor's Name	Time In	Time Out	Reason for Visit	Signature

Date	Visitor's Name	Time In	Time Out	Reason for Visit	Signature

Date	Visitor's Name	Time In	Time Out	Reason for Visit	Signature

Date	Visitor's Name	Time In	Time Out	Reason for Visit	Signature

Date	Visitor's Name	Time In	Time Out	Reason for Visit	Signature

Date	Visitor's Name	Time In	Time Out	Reason for Visit	Signature

Date	Visitor's Name	Time In	Time Out	Reason for Visit	Signature

Date	Visitor's Name	Time In	Time Out	Reason for Visit	Signature

Date	Visitor's Name	Time In	Time Out	Reason for Visit	Signature

Date	Visitor's Name	Time In	Time Out	Reason for Visit	Signature

Date	Visitor's Name	Time In	Time Out	Reason for Visit	Signature

Date	Visitor's Name	Time In	Time Out	Reason for Visit	Signature

Date	Visitor's Name	Time In	Time Out	Reason for Visit	Signature

Date	Visitor's Name	Time In	Time Out	Reason for Visit	Signature

Date	Visitor's Name	Time In	Time Out	Reason for Visit	Signature

Date	Visitor's Name	Time In	Time Out	Reason for Visit	Signature

Date	Visitor's Name	Time In	Time Out	Reason for Visit	Signature

Date	Visitor's Name	Time In	Time Out	Reason for Visit	Signature

Date	Visitor's Name	Time In	Time Out	Reason for Visit	Signature

Date	Visitor's Name	Time In	Time Out	Reason for Visit	Signature

Date	Visitor's Name	Time In	Time Out	Reason for Visit	Signature

Date	Visitor's Name	Time In	Time Out	Reason for Visit	Signature

Date	Visitor's Name	Time In	Time Out	Reason for Visit	Signature

Date	Visitor's Name	Time In	Time Out	Reason for Visit	Signature

Date	Visitor's Name	Time In	Time Out	Reason for Visit	Signature

Date	Visitor's Name	Time In	Time Out	Reason for Visit	Signature

Date	Visitor's Name	Time In	Time Out	Reason for Visit	Signature

Date	Visitor's Name	Time In	Time Out	Reason for Visit	Signature

Date	Visitor's Name	Time In	Time Out	Reason for Visit	Signature

Date	Visitor's Name	Time In	Time Out	Reason for Visit	Signature

Date	Visitor's Name	Time In	Time Out	Reason for Visit	Signature

Date	Visitor's Name	Time In	Time Out	Reason for Visit	Signature

Date	Visitor's Name	Time In	Time Out	Reason for Visit	Signature

Date	Visitor's Name	Time In	Time Out	Reason for Visit	Signature
Date	Visitor's Name	Time In	Time Out	Reason for Visit	Signature

Date	Visitor's Name	Time In	Time Out	Reason for Visit	Signature

Date	Visitor's Name	Time In	Time Out	Reason for Visit	Signature

Date	Visitor's Name	Time In	Time Out	Reason for Visit	Signature

Date	Visitor's Name	Time In	Time Out	Reason for Visit	Signature

Date	Visitor's Name	Time In	Time Out	Reason for Visit	Signature

Date	Visitor's Name	Time In	Time Out	Reason for Visit	Signature

Date	Visitor's Name	Time In	Time Out	Reason for Visit	Signature

Date	Visitor's Name	Time In	Time Out	Reason for Visit	Signature

Date	Visitor's Name	Time In	Time Out	Reason for Visit	Signature

Date	Visitor's Name	Time In	Time Out	Reason for Visit	Signature

Date	Visitor's Name	Time In	Time Out	Reason for Visit	Signature

Date	Visitor's Name	Time In	Time Out	Reason for Visit	Signature

Date	Visitor's Name	Time In	Time Out	Reason for Visit	Signature

Date	Visitor's Name	Time In	Time Out	Reason for Visit	Signature

Date	Visitor's Name	Time In	Time Out	Reason for Visit	Signature

Date	Visitor's Name	Time In	Time Out	Reason for Visit	Signature

Date	Visitor's Name	Time In	Time Out	Reason for Visit	Signature

Date	Visitor's Name	Time In	Time Out	Reason for Visit	Signature

Date	Visitor's Name	Time In	Time Out	Reason for Visit	Signature

Date	Visitor's Name	Time In	Time Out	Reason for Visit	Signature

Date	Visitor's Name	Time In	Time Out	Reason for Visit	Signature

Date	Visitor's Name	Time In	Time Out	Reason for Visit	Signature

Date	Visitor's Name	Time In	Time Out	Reason for Visit	Signature

Date	Visitor's Name	Time In	Time Out	Reason for Visit	Signature

Date	Visitor's Name	Time In	Time Out	Reason for Visit	Signature

Date	Visitor's Name	Time In	Time Out	Reason for Visit	Signature

Date	Visitor's Name	Time In	Time Out	Reason for Visit	Signature

Date	Visitor's Name	Time In	Time Out	Reason for Visit	Signature

Date	Visitor's Name	Time In	Time Out	Reason for Visit	Signature

Date	Visitor's Name	Time In	Time Out	Reason for Visit	Signature

Date	Visitor's Name	Time In	Time Out	Reason for Visit	Signature

Date	Visitor's Name	Time In	Time Out	Reason for Visit	Signature

Date	Visitor's Name	Time In	Time Out	Reason for Visit	Signature

Date	Visitor's Name	Time In	Time Out	Reason for Visit	Signature

Date	Visitor's Name	Time In	Time Out	Reason for Visit	Signature

Date	Visitor's Name	Time In	Time Out	Reason for Visit	Signature

Date	Visitor's Name	Time In	Time Out	Reason for Visit	Signature

Date	Visitor's Name	Time In	Time Out	Reason for Visit	Signature

Date	Visitor's Name	Time In	Time Out	Reason for Visit	Signature

Date	Visitor's Name	Time In	Time Out	Reason for Visit	Signature

Date	Visitor's Name	Time In	Time Out	Reason for Visit	Signature

Date	Visitor's Name	Time In	Time Out	Reason for Visit	Signature

Date	Visitor's Name	Time In	Time Out	Reason for Visit	Signature

Date	Visitor's Name	Time In	Time Out	Reason for Visit	Signature
Date	Visitor's Name	Time In	Time Out	Reason for Visit	Signature

Date	Visitor's Name	Time In	Time Out	Reason for Visit	Signature

Date	Visitor's Name	Time In	Time Out	Reason for Visit	Signature

Date	Visitor's Name	Time In	Time Out	Reason for Visit	Signature

Date	Visitor's Name	Time In	Time Out	Reason for Visit	Signature

Date	Visitor's Name	Time In	Time Out	Reason for Visit	Signature

Date	Visitor's Name	Time In	Time Out	Reason for Visit	Signature

Date	Visitor's Name	Time In	Time Out	Reason for Visit	Signature

Date	Visitor's Name	Time In	Time Out	Reason for Visit	Signature

Date	Visitor's Name	Time In	Time Out	Reason for Visit	Signature

Date	Visitor's Name	Time In	Time Out	Reason for Visit	Signature

Date	Visitor's Name	Time In	Time Out	Reason for Visit	Signature

Date	Visitor's Name	Time In	Time Out	Reason for Visit	Signature

Date	Visitor's Name	Time In	Time Out	Reason for Visit	Signature

Date	Visitor's Name	Time In	Time Out	Reason for Visit	Signature

Date	Visitor's Name	Time In	Time Out	Reason for Visit	Signature

Date	Visitor's Name	Time In	Time Out	Reason for Visit	Signature

Date	Visitor's Name	Time In	Time Out	Reason for Visit	Signature

Date	Visitor's Name	Time In	Time Out	Reason for Visit	Signature

Date	Visitor's Name	Time In	Time Out	Reason for Visit	Signature

Date	Visitor's Name	Time In	Time Out	Reason for Visit	Signature

Date	Visitor's Name	Time In	Time Out	Reason for Visit	Signature

Date	Visitor's Name	Time In	Time Out	Reason for Visit	Signature

Date	Visitor's Name	Time In	Time Out	Reason for Visit	Signature

Date	Visitor's Name	Time In	Time Out	Reason for Visit	Signature

Date	Visitor's Name	Time In	Time Out	Reason for Visit	Signature

Date	Visitor's Name	Time In	Time Out	Reason for Visit	Signature

Date	Visitor's Name	Time In	Time Out	Reason for Visit	Signature

Date	Visitor's Name	Time In	Time Out	Reason for Visit	Signature

Date	Visitor's Name	Time In	Time Out	Reason for Visit	Signature

www.ingramcontent.com/pod-product-compliance
Lightning Source LLC
Chambersburg PA
CBHW081113180526
45170CB00008B/2825